FOR ANATOLE'S TOMB

STÉPHANE MALLARMÉ (1842-98) was born in Paris, the city where he lived for much of his life, and where he died. He worked as an English teacher for many years. His early poetry was influenced by Baudelaire, and throughout his life he was centrally involved in the development of French Symbolism through his close association with writers such as André Gide, Paul Valéry, and Paul Verlaine. He also had contacts with the artistic and musical world; most notably his poem *L'après-midi d'un faune* inspired Debussy's tone poem of the same title, and was illustrated by Manet.

PATRICK MCGUINNESS is a Fellow of St Anne's College, Oxford, where he lectures in French. In 1998 he won an Eric Gregory award for poetry from the Society of Authors, and his poems and translations have appeared in *The Independent*, *Leviathan*, the *London Review of Books*, *Picador New Writing*, *PN Review* and *Poetry Wales*. A selection of his poetry appears in *New Poetries II* (Carcanet, 1999). His books include *T.E. Hulme: Selected Writings* (Carcanet, 1998), *Maurice Maeterlinck and the Making of Modern Theatre* (OUP, 2000), *Symbolism, Decadence and the fin de siècle* (University of Exeter Press), an edition of Laura Riding and Robert Graves, *A Survey of Modernist Poetry* (Carcanet, 2002) and *Anthologie de la poésie symboliste et décadente* (Les Belles Lettres, 2001).

Fyfield*Books* aim to make available some of the great classics of British and European literature in clear, affordable formats, and to restore often neglected writers to their place in literary tradition.

Fyfield*Books* take their name from the Fyfield elm in Matthew Arnold's 'Scholar Gypsy' and 'Thyrsis'. The tree stood not far from the village where the series was originally devised in 1971.

> *Roam on! The light we sought is shining still.*
> *Dost thou ask proof? Our tree yet crowns the hill,*
> *Our Scholar travels yet the loved hill-side*

from 'Thyrsis'

STÉPHANE MALLARMÉ

For Anatole's Tomb

Translated with an introduction and afterword by
PATRICK McGUINNESS

ROUTLEDGE
New York

Published in USA and Canada in 2003 by
Routledge
29 West 35th Street
New York, NY 10001
www.routledge-ny.com

Routledge is an imprint of the Taylor & Francis Group.

By arrangement with Carcanet Press Ltd.

First published in Great Britain
by Carcanet Press Ltd in 2003

Translation, introduction and afterword Copyright
© Patrick McGuinness 2003

Cataloguing-in-Publication data is available from the Library of Congress.

ISBN 0-415-96767-8

Printed and bound by SRP Limited, England

CONTENTS

ACKNOWLEDGEMENTS AND
NOTE ON THE TEXT

The translation is based on the text established by Bertrand Marchal in the Pléiade edition of volume I (pp. 513–45) of Mallarmé's *Œuvres complètes* (Paris: Gallimard, 1998). I am grateful to Bertrand Marchal who kindly advised me on the text and on the permissions.

Mallarmé's notes, kept in the Bibliothèque littéraire Jacques Doucet in Paris, are hand-written in pencil on 210 sheets of paper, of which all but one are 12.5 by 7.5 centimetres in size. The numbers in square brackets above the text in the original French designate the sheet numbers of Mallarmé's hand-written manuscript. Where, also in the French, a number in square brackets is embedded in a paragraph or sequence of text, it designates the consecutive sheets that make up that particular sequence.

A different version of 'Mallarmé and the *Tombeau d'Anatole*' appeared in *Situating Mallarmé*, edited by David Kinloch and Gordon Millan (Oxford: Peter Lang, 2000), and parts of the translation have appeared in the *London Review of Books* and *PN Review*.

I am grateful to David Cram, Sara James, Alan Raitt and John Redmond for their comments and suggestions, and to Judith Willson for help with the preparation of this book.

Patrick McGuinness

INTRODUCTION

In October 1879, Mallarmé's eight-year-old son Anatole died after several months of illness. The child dips in and out of the *Correspondance* like a thread, now visible, now lost, along the father's letters to his friends and fellow-poets between 1871 and 1879. At times alive and well, demanding, *turbulent* both in and out of the womb, and at times sick, quiet, withdrawn, Anatole soon emerges as a regular figure in the recurring *dramatis personae* of his father's letters. These *dramatis personae* include the poet's wife, Marie, and his daughter Geneviève, but also – and here too we find characters whose coming into the world is fraught, painful, triumphant – the likes of Hérodiade and the *faune*, the speaker-subjects of two of Malllarmé's major works, *Hérodiade* and *L'Après-midi d'un faune*. Mallarmé's letters provide a great deal of information about the development of these poems, but tell us nothing of the 210 sheets of pencilled notes towards a poem about the death of Anatole. These notes did not appear in Mallarmé's lifetime, and there are no references to a work in progress in his correspondence. When they were first published in 1961 by Jean-Pierre Richard under the title *Pour un tombeau d'Anatole*, they revealed a side of Mallarmé thereto largely unknown, and which even now disturbs the idea of the poet of pristine impersonality and detachment.[1] The text used for this translation is Bertrand Marchal's 1998 Pléiade edition of volume I of Mallarmé's works, which provides a definitive text and a transcription of the notes, though which differs in parts from Richard's transcription and interpretation.

Mallarmé was an expert writer of *tombeau* poems, and his great *tombeaux* for Edgar Allan Poe, Baudelaire and Verlaine combined elegy with memorial, separating the poets' troubled biographies from the permanence of the work they left behind. These notes however provide the clearest indication of why this *tombeau* for Anatole could not be written. Caught between accepting, as a poet, the boy's death, and resisting, as a father, the death of a son, Mallarmé finds two impulses – the paternal and the poetic – at odds with each other: the father mourns the life and fights the death, while the poet, 'complicit' with illness and death, prepares to write the *tombeau*. *For Anatole's Tomb* takes us to the centre of these conflicting imperatives, and shows how, when the two are ranged against each other, they make the poet's work suspect and taint the father's mourning. Mallarmé's mother had died when he was seven, and his sister Maria when he was fifteen. When Anatole died the Mallarmés had to take out a family plot in Samoreau cemetery. For Stéphane, seeing his son precede him into the grave was a dreadful reversal of the natural order, part of a protracted, transgenerational catastrophe: he had lost his mother, his sibling and now his son. As he writes in the notes for Anatole's *tombeau*: 'did not know mother, and son did not know me! – image of me other than me carried off in death!' Geneviève Mallarmé remembers her father once saying that it had been easier for Victor Hugo, since he could write about his daughter's death; he, however, could not: 'Hugo… is fortunate to have been able to speak, for me it is impossible.'[2]

Mallarmé is a poet associated with silence, though rarely with the silence of unwritable grief. What strikes first of all about the notes for Anatole's *tombeau* is the effort of will expended in the intellectual and emotional search for a position from which to begin writing. The resulting notes constitute less something unfinished than something unbegun, but for all its fragmentation *For Anatole's Tomb* is a powerful and coherent (and in many ways complete) reading experience. Its very brokenness may in the end mirror the thought behind this composition, thought which is at once in dialogue and in conflict with itself. *For Anatole's Tomb* confronts the things that stop poetry from being written, as Anatole's death puts up fierce resistance to being poeticised, even by a poet whose other *tombeau* poems are masterpieces of imagined resurrections, new lives, afterlives and defiances of death. In the *tombeaux* written for fellow-poets (notably Poe, Baudelaire, Verlaine, and Gautier) Mallarmé attempted to reconfigure death as a transient, flickering moment of betweenness. 'As into Himself at last eternity changes him', he had written of Poe, imagining the poet's death as a rite of passage on the way to Becoming. But with Anatole it is different; he has been taken, too young to make his mark on the world and too soon to become a poet and (as Mallarmé imagines) 'continue father's work'. Although one of the sheets reads 'change of mode of being that is all', *For Anatole's Tomb* remains incapable of making poetic sense of the boy's death.

The poet who sought the 'Orphic explanation of the world' expresses in these pages his 'fury against the formless'. Mallarmé sought a reader with 'a mind open to multiple comprehension', and it is one of his many paradoxes that his poetry should promise, on the one hand, dazzling feats of abolition and, on the other, a dazzling proliferation of meanings. 'To name an object is to eliminate three quarters of a poem's pleasure [...]; *to suggest* it, this is the dream', he famously wrote, and it is a dictum which has come to stand for many of the ambitions and achievements of French Symbolism. Yet unlike many of his Symbolist contemporaries, Mallarmé was not a poet of vagueness, of half-tones and pastel shades (like Verlaine), nor of the intermittently perceived, imprecisely expressed (like Maeterlinck, whose theatre of silence he was among the first to call attention to).[3] Mallarmé is not 'suggestive' in these senses, but on the contrary relentlessly and unnervingly *assertive*. In any stanza of his poetry or any paragraph of his prose, meanings are generated and juggled and cast aside, clauses and subclauses, themes and motifs are begun only to be stretched and intercalated and spliced, all unfolding at different speeds and in different directions. It is the poetry of the undecidable, not poetry for the indecisive.

With Mallarmé, the blank page, the page's native emptiness, is no neutral backdrop. This is most evident in his last great experimental poem *Un coup de dés jamais n'abolira le hasard* (*A Throw of the Dice Will Never Abolish Chance*), where it teems with promise and energy, takes a share in the poem's meanings, but at the same time threatens the blankness of total cancellation. There are few Mallarmé poems that do not draw form from absence and negativity; the first word of the first poem of his *Poésies* (the ambiguous greeting-cum-leavetaking 'Salut') is 'Rien' – 'Nothing'. When W.S. Graham wrote of 'Having to construct the silence first / To speak out on',[4] or when Samuel Beckett asserted that 'it is better to write NOTHING than not to write at all',[5] Mallarmé would have known what they meant. He knew that the act of composition must extend into the blankness that surrounds and threatens all acts of the mind, from which all such acts spring and to which they all return. As he wrote in the preface to *A Throw of the Dice*: 'the paper intervenes'.

Notes

1 *Pour un tombeau d'Anatole* (Paris: Seuil, 1961).
2 *Nouvelle revue française*, 1 December 1926, p. 521.
3 For a selection of French Symbolist poetry see Patrick McGuinness, *Anthologie de la poésie symboliste et décadente* (Paris: Les Belles Lettres, 2001).
4 'Approaches to How They Behave', *Collected Poems 1942–1977* (London: Faber and Faber, 1979), p. 174.
5 Beckett, *Disjecta* (London: Calder, 1983), p. 171.

Pour un tombeau d'Anatole

For Anatole's Tomb

X

enfant sorti de nous deux – nous montrant notre idéal, le
chemin – à nous! père et mère qui lui survivons en triste
existence, comme les deux extrêmes – mal associés en lui et
qui se sont séparés – d'où sa mort – annulant ce petit «soi»
d'enfant

malade au printemps mort et automne – c'est le soleil
——
la vague idée la toux
2)

fils résorbé pas parti
c'est lui – ou son frère
moi je le lui ai dit deux frères –

refoulée restée en flanc – sûr de moi
siècle ne s'écoulera pas
juste pour m'instruire.

fureur contre informe

X

child sprung from us both – showing us our ideal, the way
– to us! father and mother who in sad existence survive him,
like the two extremes – ill-matched in him and sundered
from each other – whence his death – abolishing this little
child 'self'

sick in the springtime dead in the autumn – it's the sun
___

the wave idea the cough
2)

son reabsorbed not gone
it is him – or his brother
I told him this two brothers –

forced back remaining in the womb – sure of myself
century will not pass by
just to instruct me.

fury against the formless

3

X

pas connu mère, et fils ne m'a pas connu! –
– image de moi autre que moi emporté en mort! –

X

ton futur qui s'est réfugié en moi devient ma pureté à travers vie, à laquelle je ne toucherai pas –

X

il est une époque de l'Existence où nous nous retrouverons, sinon un lieu –
– et si vous en doutez le monde en sera témoin, en supposant que je vive assez vieux ——

X   préf.

père qui né en temps mauvais – avait préparé à fils – une tâche sublime –
a la double à remplir – il a fait la sienne – la douleur le défie de se sacrifier à qui n'est plus – l'emportera-t-elle sur vigueur (homme qu'il n'a pas été) et fera-t-il la tâche de l'enfant

4

X

did not know mother, and son did not know me! –
– image of me other than me carried off in death! –

X

your future which has taken refuge in me becomes my
purity through life, which I shall not touch –

X

there is a time in Existence in which we will find each other
again, if not a place –
– and if you doubt that the world will be the witness,
supposing I live to be old enough ——

X   pref.

father who born in a bad time – had prepared for son – a
sublime task –
has the double one to fulfil – he fulfilled his – pain challenges
him to sacrifice himself to who is no more – will it triumph
over strength (the man he did not become) and will he do
the child's task

5

X

le but suprême n'eût été que partir pur de la vie
tu l'as accompli d'avance en souffrant assez – doux enfant
– pour que cela te soit compté pour ta vie perdue – les tiens
ont acheté le reste par leur souffrance de ne plus t'avoir

[ff⁰ˢ 12, 13]

[1]   XX

prier morts (non pour eux) –
genoux, enfant
genoux – besoin d'y avoir l'enfant – son absence – genoux
tombent – et [2] mains se joignent vers celui qu'on ne peut
presser – mais qui est –
– qu'un espace sépare ——

——

car de vrais morts qu'enfant!

[ff⁰ˢ 14, 15, 16]

[1]   X   Préf.

chéri – grand cœur – bien fils de père don't le cœur battit
pour projets trop grands – et venus là échouer
il fallait – héritant de cette merveilleuse intelligence filiale,
la [2] faisant revivre – construire avec sa lucidité – cette
œuvre – trop vaste pour moi
et ainsi, (me privant de la vie, la sacrifiant, si ce [3] n'est pour
l'œ –
– être lui grand, – et faire cela sans crainte de *jouer* avec sa
mort – puisque je lui sacrifiais ma vie – puisque j'acceptais
quant à moi – cette mort (claustration)

X

the supreme goal would have been only to leave life pure
you fulfilled this in advance by suffering enough – sweet
child – so that this may be counted for your lost life – your
family have bought the rest by their suffering at no longer
having you

XX

pray to the dead (not for them) –
knees, child
knees – need the child to be there – his absence – knees fall
– and hands join towards the one we cannot hold – but who
is –
– whom a space separates ——
——

for no real death but a child's!

X   Pref.

dear one – great heart – truly son of father whose heart beat
for projects too great – and which came there to fail
it was necessary – inheriting this marvellous filial intelligence,
making it live again – to build with his lucidity – this
work – too great for me
and thus, (robbing me of life, sacrificing it, if it is not for the
wk –
– be him grown up,– and do that without fear of *playing*
with his death – since I sacrificed my life to him – since I
accepted for my own part – this death (claustration)

7

X

exemple
nous avons su par toi ce «meilleur de nous-mêmes» qui
souvent nous échappe – et sera en nous – en nos actes,
maintentant ——
enfant, semence idéalisation

X

père et mère se promettant de n'avoir pas d'autre enfant
– fosse creusée par lui
vie cesse là

X

remèdes vains laissés
——

si nature n'a pas voulu –
j'en trouverai moi pour mort
——

baumes, seulement, consolations pour nous – doute
puis non! leur réalité

enfant – notre immortalité en effet, fait d'espoirs humains
enfouis – fils – confiés à la femme par l'homme désespérant
après jeunesse de trouver le mystère et prenant femme ——

X

example
we have known through you this 'best of ourselves'
which often escapes us – and will be in us – in our acts,
now ——
child, seed idealisation

X

father and mother vowing to have no other child
– grave dug by him
life stops there

X

vain remedies abandoned
——

if nature did not wish it –
I will find one myself for death
——

balms, only, consolations for us – doubt
then no! their reality

child – our immortality indeed, made of human hopes
buried – son – confided to the woman by the man despairing
after youth of finding the mystery and taking a wife ——

[1] malade depuis le jour où mort s'installe – marqué par maladie – n'est plus lui déjà, mais est celui qu'à travers la mort plus tard on voudrait revoir – résumant mort et corruption – apparu tel, avec son mal es sa pâleur *[2]* (malade – être à nu comme l'enfant –) et nous apparaissant – l'on profite de ces heures, où mort frappé il vit encore, et est encore à nous
titre poésie de la maladie.

à A.
hymen père et fils –
peut-être en vers

[1] j'aurais pu avec don de parole te faire roi toi, faire de toi l'enfant de l'œ, au lieu du fils en nous – de jadis
or il prouve qu'il le fut – joua ce rôle!
– non, triste
– te faire
non souviens-toi des jours mauvais – bouche fermée, etc.
parole natale oubliée – etc.
c'est moi qui t'ai aidé depuis *[2]* – ai ramené en toi l'enfant –
jeunesse ou mot de l'histoire apprise oubliée
d'où rien
je n'aurais pas souffert – en être – à mon tour n'étudier que cela – etc. (mort
[3] alors – tu ne fus donc que moi – puisque je suis ici
– seul, triste –
– non, je me souviens d'une enfance –
– la tienne.

sick from the day when death settles – marked by sickness
– is already no longer himself, but the one who through
death we would later want to see again – resuming death
and corruption – appearing thus, with his sickness and his
pallor (sick – to be naked like the child –) and appearing to
us – we make make the most of these hours, where dead
struck down he lives still, and is still ours
title poetry of sickness.

to A.
hymen father and son –
perhaps in verse

with gift of words I could have made you king you, made
you the child of the wk. instead of the son in us – of before
so it proves that he was – played that role
– no, sad
– made you
no remember the bad days – mouth closed etc. word of birth
forgotten etc.
it is I who have helped you since – have brought the child
back in you –
youth or word of story learned forgotten
whence nothing
I will not have suffered – being part of it – in my turn
studying only that – etc. (death
so – you were only me then – since I am here – alone, sad –
– no, I remember a childhood –
– yours.

deux voix)
[4] avant de faire ses classes)
ainsi c'est moi, Moire maudite – qui t'ai légué! – silence il
pardonne)
[5] Oh! Laisse… nous sur ce mot – qui nous confond tous
deux – nous unit enfin – car qui l'a dit la tienne)

———

mai sans toi je n'eusse – su

[ff^{os} 29, 35]

[1] Manipulations etc. cruelles
Oh! permets – non tu veux encore…

———

egypte ancienne – embaumement – jours, opérations
cryptes – tout ce changement, *[2]* jadis barbare et extérieur
– matériel – maintenant moral et en nous

[f° 34]

veux déjouer mort

———

entend pleurs de femme
Oh! je le reconnais tu es forte, habile – etc.

[f° 33]

frère sœur
non jamais l'*absent* ne sera moins que le présent –

two voices)
before going to his classes)
so it is me, cursed Silk – I have bequeathed you! – silence
(he forgives)
Oh! Leave… us on that word – which merges us both –
unites us at last – for who called it yours)

––––

but without you I would not have – known

cruel trappings etc.
Oh! allow – no you still want…

––––

ancient egypt – embalment – days, operations crypts – all
this change, once barbaric and external – material – now
spiritual and in us

want to cheat death

––––

hear woman's tears
Oh! I know it you are strong, capable – etc.

brother sister
no never will the *absent one* be any less than present –

sentir éclater en nuit le vide immense produit par ce qui serait sa *vie* – parce qu'il ne le *sait* pas – qu'il est mort éclair?
crise
douleur

[1] moment où il faut rompre avec le souvenir vivant, pour l'ensevelir – le mettre en bière, le cacher – avec les brutalités de la mise en bière contact rude, etc. *[2]* pour ne plus le voir qu'idéalisé – après, non plus lui vivant là – mais germe de son être repris en soi – germe permettant de penser pour lui – de le voir *[3]* vision (idéalité de l'état) et de parler pour lui – car en nous, pur lui, épuration – devenu notre honneur, la *source* de nos meilleurs sentiments – etc.
[4] [titre vraie rentrée en l'idéal]
——

coup de traîtrise de mort – du mal X sans qu'il en sache rien –
– à mon tour à la jouer, par cela même qu'enfant ignore

temps de la chambre vide – jusqu'à ce qu'on l'ouvre
peut-être tout suivre ainsi (moralement) ——

feel the immense void produced by what would be his *life* exploding into night – because he does not *know* it – that he is dead lightning flash?
attack
pain

moment when we must break with the living memory, to bury him – put him in the coffin, hide him – with the brutalities of the laying in the coffin rough contact, etc. no longer to see him except idealised – after, no longer him alive there – but seed of his being taken back into itself – seed allowing us to think for him – to see him vision (ideality of the state) and to speak for him – for in us, pure him, purification – become our honour, the *source* of our finest feelings – etc.
[title true return into the ideal]
——

treacherous blow of death – of X sickness without his knowing anything –
– my turn to cheat it, by what the child does not know

time of the empty room – until we open it perhaps everything
to follow in this way (spiritually) ——

15

il n'en sait rien! – et mère pleure – idée là
oui, prenons tout sur nous, ô toi sa vie – etc. –
car sinistre ne pas savoir en n'être plus.

[1] Tu peux, avec tes petites mains, m'entraîner dans ta
tombe – tu en as le droit –
– moi-même qui te suis uni, je me laisse aller –
– mais si tu veux, à nous deux faisons… [2] une alliance –
un hymen, superbe – et la vie restant en moi je m'en servirai
pour…
donc pas mère alors?

[1] cérémonie – cercueil – etc.
on a vu là (le père) tout le côté matériel – qui permet de se
dire au besoin – eh! bien oui! tout est là – pas de crainte pour
moi de penser à autre chose (la reformation [2] de son esprit,
qui a l'éternité – peut attendre (soit mais éternité à travers
ma vie)
_____
père –
former son esprit (lui absent, hélas! comme on l'eût formé
lui présent mieux mais [3] parfois quand tout semble trop
bien aller – ainsi en idéal – s'écrier – du ton de mère, qui elle
est devenue attentive – Ce n'est pas tout cela
je le veux, *lui* – et non moi –

16

he has no idea! – and mother weeps – idea there
yes, let us take everything upon us, o you his life – etc. –
for terrible not to know and no longer be.

You can, with your little hands, drag me into your grave –
you have the right –
– I myself who am joined with you, I let myself go –
– but if you wish, the two of us, let us make… an alliance –
a hymen, magnificent – and the life left in me I will use
to …
– so not mother then?

ceremony – coffin – etc.
there we saw (the father) the whole material side – which
lets us tell ourselves at need – ah! well yes! it is all there –
no fear for me thinking of something else (the reformation
of his spirit, which is eternal – can wait (granted but eternity
through my life)

––––

father –
shape his spirit (he absent, alas! as we would have shaped
him better present but sometimes when it all seems to be
going too well – as in ideal – cry out – in the mother's tone,
she who has become attentive – This is not enough
I want him, *him* – and not me –

[1] tu me regardes
Je ne peux pas te dire encore la vérité
je n'ose, trop petit
Ce qui t'est arrivé – Un jour je te le dirai – car *homme* je ne
veux pas [2] que tu ne saches pas ton sort – et homme enfant
mort

non – pas mêlé aux grands morts – etc. – tant que nous
mêmes vivons, il vit – en nous –
ce n'est qu'après notre mort qu'il en sera – et que les cloches
des Morts sonneront pour lui

     (I
petite vierge
fiancée vie qui eût été une femme
––––
que je te conte à quoi tu manques – mais

Oh! laissez – nous fumerions pipe – et causerions de ce qu'à
nous deux nous savons mystère

voile – navigue
fleuve, ta vie qui passe, coule –

you look at me
I cannot yet tell you the truth
I dare not, too little
What has happened to you – One day I will tell you – for
man I do not want you not to know your fate – and man dead
child

no – not among the great dead – etc. – so long as we
ourselves live, he lives – in us
only after our death will he be – and will the bells of the
Dead toll for him

       (I
little virgin
betrothed life who would have been a woman
———
let me tell you about what you are missing from – but

Oh! leave – we would have smoked pipe – would have
talked of what we both knew mystery

sail – navigate
river, your life passing, flows –

[f° 52]

Oh! fais-nous souffrir toi qui ne t'en doutes pas beaucoup –
tout ce qui équivaut à ta vie brisée, douloureuse en nous –
tandis qu'alors tu planes, libre

[f° 53]

Quoi! ce jour des morts – pour lui – lui –

[f° 54]

Le sacrifie de l'enfant pour que terre – mère – tâche cité
hommes

[f° 55]

fin de I
– ô terreur il est mort! –
il *est*... mort (absolument – c. à d. frappé
la mère le voit tel –
de façon à ce que, malade, il semble revenir – ou se revoir
en le futur – obtenu au présent

[ff° 56, 57]

mère I
on ne peut pas mourir avec de pareils yeux, etc. –
père laisse entendre en son effroi, sanglots «il est mort»
– et c'est en vague de ce cri, que II l'enfant se [2] lève sur son
lit – se cherche, etc. –
et III peut-être rien – sur mort et donné à entendre simplement
– en l'espace de «il est mort de I II
———

20

Oh! make us suffer you who have so little idea –
all that amounts to your broken life, painful in us –
while then you glide, free

What! this day of the dead – for him – him –

The sacrifice of the child so that earth – mother – task city
men

end of I
– O terror he is dead! –
– he *is*… dead (absolutely – i.e. stricken
mother sees him thus
in such a way that, sick, he seems to come back – or to see
himself again in the future – obtained in the present

mother I
no one can die with such eyes, etc. –
father lets out in his terror, sobs 'he is dead'
– and it is in the wake of that cry, that II the child sits up in
his bed – looks around, etc. –
and III perhaps nothing – about death and simply implied
– in the space of 'he is dead of I II
——

Le père cherche – et s'arrête – l'enfant étant là, encore,
comme pour ressaisir la vie – or interruption chez le père –
et la mère apparue espoirs soins – le double côté homme
femme – tantôt chez l'un, chez l'autre, d'où union profonde

[1] et toi sa sœur, toi qui un jour – (ce gouffre ouvert depuis
sa mort et qui nous suivra jusqu'à la nôtre – quand nous y
serons descendus ta mère et moi) dois un jour [2] nous
réunir tous trois en ta pensée, ta mémoire
———
– de même qu'en une seule tombe
toi qui, selon l'ordre, viendras sur cette tombe, non faite
pour toi –

      Pr

Soleil couché et vent
or parti, et vent de *rien qui souffle* (là, le néant moderne)?

larmes, afflux de lucidité, le mort se revoit à travers ——

22

The father searches – and stops – the child being there, still, as if to take hold of life again – hence interruption in the father – and the mother appearing hopes cares – the double side man woman – first with the one, then the other, hence deep union

and you his sister, you who one day – (this gulf open since his death and which will follow us to ours – when we have gone down your mother and I) must one day reunite all three of us in your thought, your memory
——
– just as in a single tomb
you who, in due time, will come upon this tomb, not made for you –

        Pr

Sun down and wind
gold gone, and wind of *nothingness blowing* (this, the modern void)?

tears, flow of lucidity, the dead one sees himself again through ——

Pr et X
[1] la Mort – chuchote bas – je ne suis personne – je m'ignore même (car morts ne savent pas qu'ils sont morts –, ni même qu'ils meurent – pour enfants du moins – ou *[2]* héros – morts soudaines – car autrement ma beauté est faite *des derniers instantes* – lucidité, beauté visage – de ce qui serait *[3]* moi, sans moi – car aussitôt que je suis – (qu'on est mort) je cesse d'être – ainsi faite de presciences, d'intuitions, frissons *[4]* suprêmes – je ne suis pas – (qu'à l'état idéal) – et pour les autres, larmes deuil, etc. – et c'est mon *[5]* ombre ignorante de moi, qui revêt de *deuil* les autres –

[1]   Notes
        ——

quoique poëme basé sur faits toujours – doive ne prendre que faits généraux – il se trouve ici que donnée d'ensemble s'accorde *[2]* souvent avec les moments derniers du délicieux enfant –
ainsi père – voyant qu'il doit être mort – mère, illusion suprême, etc.

mort – épuration image en *nous* épurés par larmes ——
et avant image aussi –
reste simplement ne pas *toucher* – mais se parler –

24

Pr and X

Death – whispers softly – I am no one – I do not even know myself (for dead do not know that they are dead –, nor even that they are dying – for children at least – or heroes – sudden deaths – for otherwise my beauty is made up *of last moments* – lucidity, beauty face – of what would be me, without me – for as soon as I am – (that one dies) I cease to be – thus made of forebodings, of intuitions, supreme shudders – I am not – (except in ideal state) – and for the others, tears mourning, etc. – and it is my shadow ignorant of me, that clothes the others in *mourning* –

Notes
___

although poem based on facts always – must only take general facts – it occurs here that guiding principle of whole often fits with the last moments of the lovely child – thus father – seeing he must be dead – mother, supreme illusion, etc.

death – purification image in *us* purified by tears —— and before image also – it remains simply not to *touch* – but speak to each other –

[1]   II   *effet général*

est-il mort? (c. à d. frappé à mort) et revient-il déjà (dans l'espace du *doit* mourir) du futur terrible qui l'attend? [2] ou bien est-il encore malade?
maladie à laquelle on se rattache; désirant qu'elle dure, pour l'avoir, lui plus longemps –
or la *mort* [3] «pourquoi m'attarder à vous le rendre inquiet – triste – déformé – tandis que je le pétris pour le jour beau et sacré où il ne souffrira plus – (sur le [4] lit de mort – mais muet, etc. – au lieu d'autrefois I – ce qui donnerait peut-être pour I – «Oh! s'il mourait jamais…
mère [5] n'achève pas –
– il faut le père et mère? qui se retrouvent tous deux devant sépulcre – sans lui
eh! bien – ?

[1] ne pas le sentir sur mes genoux, assis, rêveur causant avec lui [,] cela fait qu'ils se dérobent et que je me suis agenouillé – non plus devant l'enfant familier etc. – alors, avec [2] sa veste – (marin?) mais devant le jeune dieu, héros, sacré par mort –

famille parfaite
équilibre père fils mère fille rompu – trois, un vide entre nous, cherchant…

II   *general effect*

is he dead? (i.e. stricken to death) and is he already returning
(in the space of the *must* die) from the terrible future that
awaits him? or is he still sick?
sickness to which we cling, wanting it to last, so we can have
him, longer –
then *death* 'why waste time giving him back to you worried
– sad – distorted – when I am shaping him for the sacred
and beautiful day when he will suffer no more – (on the
death bed – but mute, etc. – instead of as before I – which
would perhaps go into I – 'Oh! if ever he died…
mother does not finish –
– needs father and mother? who find themselves together
before sepulchre – without him
ah! then – ?

not to feel him on my knees, sitting, daydreaming talking
with him, that means they disappear and that I have knelt
down – no longer before the familiar child etc. – then, with
his jacket – (sailor?) but before the young god, hero,
sanctified by death –

perfect family
equilibrium father son mother daughter broken – three, a
void between us, searching…

tant mieux qu'il ne le sache pas – nous prenons toutes
larmes – pleure, mère
etc. – transition d'un état à l'autre
ainsi pas mort
mort – ridicule ennemie – qui ne peux à l'enfant infliger la
notion que tu es!

mort n'est rien
prière de *mère* – jouant mort elle
«que l'enfant ne sache pas –
et père en profite.

plus de *vie* pour moi et je me sens couché en la tombe à côté
de toi –

ou: Poème ordinaire
C'est vrai – tu m'as frappé et tu as bien choisi ta blessure –
– etc. – mais
———
et vengeance lutte d'un génie et de la mort

best that he not know – we take all the tears – weep, mother
etc. – transition from one state to the other
thus not dead
death – ridiculous enemy – unable to inflict upon the child
the notion that you are!

death is nothing
prayer of *mother* – she cheating death
'let the child not know –
and the father makes the most of it.

no more *life* for me and I feel myself lying in the grave beside
you –

or: ordinary Poem
It is true – you have struck me and you have chosen your
wound well –
– etc. – but
____

and vengeance struggle of a spirit and of death

[1] Mort

il n'est que des consolations, pensées – baume mais ce qui est fait est fait – on ne peut revenir sur l'absolu contenu en mort –

– et cependant montrer que si, abstraction faite *[2]* de vie, de bonheur d'être ensemble, etc. – cette consolation a son tour, a son fonds – sa base – absolus – en ce que (si nous voulons par exemple qu'un être mort vive en nous, pensée – c'est son être, sa *[3]* pensée en effet – ce qu'il a de meilleur qui arrive, par notre amour et le soin que nous prenons à l'être – (être, n'étant que moral et quant à pensée) il y a là un au delà magnifique *[4]* qui retrouve sa vérité – d'autant plus pure et belle que la rupture absolue de la mort – devenue peu à peu aussi illusoire qu'absolue (d'où il est permis de paraître oublier les douleurs etc. –) *[5]* – comme cet illusoire de survie en nous, devient d'illusoire absolu – (il y a *irréalité* dans les deux cas) a été terrible et vraie,

———

le père seul la mère seule – se cachant l'un de l'autre et cela se retrouve… ensemble

ô terre – tu n'as pas une plante – à quoi bon –
– moi qui t'honore –
bouquets vaine beauté

doigt mystérieux montré
les amis apparus – chassant les faux ———

Dead
there are only consolations, thoughts – balm but what is done is done – we cannot go back on the absolute contained in death –
– and yet to show that if, with life gone, happiness of being together, etc. – this consolation in its turn has its foundation – its grounds – absolute – in the fact that (if for instance we want a dead being to live in us, thought – it is their being, their thought in effect – what is best in them that comes, by our love and the care we take in being them – (being, being only moral and taking place in thought) there is here a magnificent beyond which rediscovers its truth – all the more beautiful and pure as the absolute rupture of death – little by little become as illusory as it is absolute (whence we are allowed to seem to forget the pain etc. –) – like the illusion of survival in us, becomes the absolute illusory – (in both cases there is *unreality*) has been terrible and real,
―――

the father alone the mother alone – hiding from each other and this leaves them… together

O earth – you have no plant – what good –
– I who honour you –
flowers vain beauty

mysterious finger pointed to
friends appeared – chasing away the false ones ――――

reste là – de source vaine mort?
soit! et que la vie passe – fleuve à côté de lui gardé par nature
sévère
————

le petit tombé dans la vallée

pureté double – identité –
les yeux
les deux points de vue égaux

ses yeux me regardent, doubles et suffisent – pris déjà par
l'absence et le gouffre –
tout y raccorder?

[1] l'homme et l'absence – l'esprit jumeau avec lequel il
s'unit quand il rêve, songe – absence, seule après mort, une
[2] fois le pieux enfouissement du corps, fait
mystérieusement – cette fiction accordée –

Le sacrifice – sur le tombeau
pourpre-roi, amour mère
il le faut – pour qu'il soit encore – ! (transfusion) mère veut
seule l'avoir, elle est terre –

stay there – from vain source death?
so be it! and let life pass – river beside him guarded by
solemn nature
―――
the little child fallen in the valley

double purity – identity –
the eyes
the two equal points of view

his two eyes are watching me, they are enough – already
taken by absence and the gulf –
bring everything to this?

man and absence – the twin spirit with which he merges
when he dreams, thinks – absence, alone after death, once
the pious burial of the body, mysteriously undertaken – this
fiction accorded –

The sacrifice – on the tomb
purple king, mother love
it is necessary – so he can be again – ! (transfusion) mother
wants to have him to herself, she is earth –

Puisqu'il *faut*
Que dis-tu là –
ne m'interromps point –

I

craintes de mère – il a cessé de jouer aujourd'hui
père écoute – voit yeux de mère – laisse soigner II et songe
lui –

II

larmes de mère
pièce
se calmant peu à peu dans le double point de vue
enfant, destinée –
tombeau, souvenir vieillard –
– (qui parle)

I   cri de mère
fleurs cueillies pour tombe, laissées là

III
tombeau
père –

Since it is *has to be*
What are you saying there –
don't interrupt me –

       I

mother's fears – he stopped playing today
father listens – sees mother's eyes – lets her tend to II
he is thinking –

       II

mother's tears
room
calming down little by little in the double perspective
child, destiny –
tomb, memory old man –
– (who is speaking)

       I   mother's cry
flowers picked for grave, left there

       III
tomb
father –

lent à sacrifice
terre le change pendant ce temps
autre mère (mère se tait?) douleur éternelle et muette.

[1] Père – s'il nous entendait qu'il serait irrité –
le supprimer ainsi sacrilège sans qu'il le sache! tombeau
ombre –
non, divinement car pas mort et en nous – la [2] transfusion
– changement de mode d'être, voilà tout

quoi! jouir de la présence et l'oublier absent – simplement!
ingratitude! non – «prise» sur l'être» de qui a été – absolu –

Amertume et besoin de vengeance quand il semble
réclamer ——
désir de ne plus rien faire – manquer le but sublime, etc. –

quoi! la mort énorme – la terrible mort – frapper un si petit
être –
je dis à la mort | lâche
hélas! elle est en nous non le dehors

slow to sacrifice
during this time earth transforms him
other mother (mother says nothing?) mute and everlasting
pain.

Father – if he could hear us how angry he would be –
sacrilege to suppress him like this without his knowing it!
tomb shadow –
no, divinely for not dead and in us – the transfusion –
change of mode of being, that is all

what! take joy in presence and forget him gone – so simply!
ingratitude! no – 'hold' on the being' of the one who has
been – absolute –

Bitterness and need for revenge when he seems to
demand ——
desire no longer to do anything – to miss the sublime goal,
etc. –

what! great death – terrible death – to strike such a small
being –
I say to death | coward
alas! it is in us not outside

il a creusé notre tombe en mourant
concession

III
Ami
– l'ami ——
ensevelissement à la vision de l'enfant
toi seul ne le sais pas – tu me regardes toujours étonné –
comment te
va – ferme ces doux yeux – ne sache pas – je me charge –
continue et tu vivras –

[1] – craintes de la mère
le voir *mort* sur lit funéraire dès la cessation de jeux en I –
fin de I
rupture
voix qui crie jusque là – pour l'enfant muet [2] et relier –
yeux fermes – père – (mère les a fermés – «ne pas savoir où
il est», l'enterrer dans l'ombre – lutte, lutte –

Oh! que les yeux des morts etc. ont plus de force que ceux,
les plus beaux des vivants – qu'ils vous attireraient
——

38

he dug our grave by dying
cemetery plot

       III
Friend
– the friend ——
burial in the child's eye
you alone do not know – you always look at me suprised –
how to
go – close those gentle eyes – never know – I will
take care of it –
continue and you will live –

– the mother's fears
see him *dead* on the funeral bed from the moment the
playing stops in I –
end of I
rupture
voice crying out until then – for the mute child and link up
– closed eyes – father – (mother has closed them – 'not to
know where he is', bury him in the shadow – struggle,
struggle –

Oh! how the eyes of the dead etc. have more power than
those, the most beautiful eyes of the living – how they would
draw you to them
——

Scission de I à III
enfant mort là
III (s'adresser souvent à lui
je te prends mon enfant, –
chambre ardente pensée – ensevelissement en ——
I et II larmes des deux cachées l'un à l'autre

III
tombeau – fatalité
– père – «il devait mourir –»
mère ne veut pas qu'on parle ainsi de son fruit –
– et père revient à destinée accomplie en tant qu'enfant

III

terre parle – mère confondue à terre par fosse creusée par
enfant – où elle sera – plus tard –

enfant
sœur reste, qui amènera un frère futur – elle exempte de
cette tombe pour père mère et fils – par son mariage.

Break between I to III
child dead here
III (speak to him often
I hold you my child, –
room of rest thought – burial in ——
I and II tears of both hidden from each other

          III
tomb – fate
– father – 'he had to die –'
mother does not want anyone to speak like this about her
fruit –
– and father returns to destiny fulfilled as child

          III

earth speaks – mother mingled with earth by grave dug by
child – where she will be – later –

child
sister remains, who will bring a future brother – she spared
from this grave ready for father mother and son – by her
marriage.

41

douleur – non larmes vaines – tombant en ignorance – mais émotion, nourrissant ton ombre qui se vivifie en nous – l'installant – tribut vivifiant pour lui –

ne pleure pas si haut il entendrait –
———
fille frappée de stupeur

Quoi! était-il donc né pour ne pas être
mère trop beau trop
et effroi chez le père maudissant son sang
– la mère – si, fait pour être, ses yeux – à quoi bon tant
d'esprit, etc. – il vivra! (cri dernier) soins, etc.
au moins mort prends le sans qu'il *[2]* le sache
ou mère (parfois, il se détourne de moi, et si terrible sacrifice
– père raccordera tout plus tard en prolongeant son être,
résorbant etc.

Père silencieux
début de pensée –
oh! l'horrible secret dont je suis possesseur (qu'en faire –
deviendrai l'ombre de son tombeau non su –
– qu'il doit mourir

42

pain – not vain tears – falling in ignorance – but emotion,
feeding your shade which comes to life in us – sustaining it
– life-giving tribute for it –

don't cry so loudly he might hear –
——
daughter struck with terror

    What! was he then born not to be
mother he was too beautiful too
and terror in father cursing his blood
– the mother – yes, made for being, his eyes – what good so
much spirit etc. – he will live! (last cry) treatments, etc.
death at least take him without his knowing
or mother (sometimes, he turns away from me, and such
terrible sacrifice
– father will redeem everything later by prolonging his
being, reabsorbing etc.

Father silent
beginning of thought –
Oh! the horrible secret I possess (what to do with it – I will
become the shadow of his unknown tomb –
– that he must die

contrecoup
éternité expirée en notre amour – il nous prolonge au delà
en nous faisant penseur – (en échange nous lui rendons vie

X

tendrement: il ne faut plus pleurer
ne *pleurons plus* te voici homme – je puis te dire ce que tu ne
sais pas que tu fus trahi – mensonge, etc. –
──
vieux athée
dieu de sa race
– comme poète pas – comme homme – celui qui remue
chacun de nos gestes etc.
– l'or!

après, non tu ne le prendras pas
Oui – je reconnais ta puissance ô mort
et tes dessous – tu l'as pris – il n'est plus qu'esprit en nous
– etc.
mais mort impuissante contre le génie humain tant
qu'humanité
siècle voix tombeau

repercussion
eternity expired in our love – he prolongs us up above by
making us thinker (in exchange we give him back life

                  X

tenderly: we must not cry any more
let us cry no more now you are a man – I can tell you what
you do not know that you were betrayed – lie etc. –
———
old atheist
god of his race
– as poet not – as man – the one who guides each of our
movements etc.
– the gold!

afterwards, no you will not take him
Yes – I acknowledge your power O death
and your plots – you took him – he is nothing but spirit in
us now – etc.
but death powerless against the human mind so long as
humanity
century voice tomb

fosse
terre – trou ouvert et jamais comblé – que par ciel
– terre indifférente
tombe
non fleurs
bouquets, nos fêtes et notre vie

[1] petit enfant que mort peut prendre l'ignorant – mais
jeune homme irrité – déjà en lui – je n'ose soutenir ce regard
plein de futur
– eh! bien, *mal [-]* de race dans moi – que ce regard suit au
delà en futur (absolu) notre réunion
faut-il – selon quel rite? l'inhumer en nom de race, ancêtres,
avec *[3]* immortalité – ou le mien nouveau –

[1]   X

cimetière
nécessaire d'y aller pour renouveler déchirure
douleur – par l'être cher
idée de là
———

quand l'illusion trop forte de l'avoir toujours avec soi *[2]*
devient une jouissance (point assez amère) pour nous – et
injuste pour celui qui reste là bas, et est *en réalité* privé de
tout ce à quoi nous l'associons. ——
———

non, tu n'es pas un mort – tu ne seras pas parmi les morts,
toujours en nous

ditch
earth – hole gaping and never filled – except by sky
– indifferent earth
grave
no flowers
bouquets, our celebrations and our life

little child whom death can take without his knowing – but
young afflicted man – already in him – I dare not endure his
gaze full of the future
– Oh! well, hereditary *illness* in me – that this gaze follows
beyond into (absolute) future our reunion
must we – by what ritual? bury him in name of race,
ancestors,
with immortality – or mine new –

X

cemetery
necessary to go there to renew laceration
pain – through the dear being
idea of there
———
when the too powerful illusion of having him always with
us becomes a delight (not bitter enough) for us – and unjust
for the one who is left there, and is *in reality* deprived of all
that we associate him with. ——
———
no, you are not one of the dead – you will not be among
the dead, always in us

mère identité de vie mort
père reprend rythme pris ici du bercement de mère
suspens – vie mort – poésie – pensée

[1] non mort – tu ne le tromperas pas –
– je profite de ce que tu le trompes – pour son heureuse
ignorance à lui – mais d'autre part je te le reprends pour le
tombeau idéal
[2] je veux tu souffrir pour toi qui ignores – rien ne sera
soustrait (qu'à toi) du deuil inouï –
et c'est moi, l'homme que tu eusses été ——
– car je vais, à [3] dater de maintenant – t'être père et mère
à deux
leur amour
idée de l'enfant
à mère
pleure toi – moi, je pense

[1]   Tombeau

        I. quoi! … ici le sanglot
la protestation indignée projetée à l'infini
        II. prendre sur soi toutes ses souffrances
moyen –
et III. alors, on peut, yeux levés au ciel –
——

tirer la ligne finale, et calme du lourd tombeau – [2]
gravement – chose si pénible avant – mais non sans (sacrifice
de jouissances?) jeter encore sur cette ligne sinistre et
d'effacement les dernières fleurs jadis pour lui regrettées

48

mother identity of life dead
father takes up rhythm begun here from mother's rocking
suspension – life death – poetry – thought

no death – you will not deceive him –
– I gain from the fact that you are deceiving him – by his
own happy ignorance – but on the other hand I take him
back from you for the ideal tomb
I want you to suffer for you who do not know – nothing will
be taken away (except from you) from the dreadful
mourning –
and it is me, the man you should have been ——
– for I will, from now onwards – be you father and mother
both
their love
idea of the child
to mother
you cry – me, I'm thinking

    Tomb

      I. what! ... here the sob
indignant protestation hurled out at the infinite
      II. take all the suffering on self
means –
and III. then, we can, eyes lifted to the sky –
——

draw the final, calm line of the heavy tombstone – solemnly
– something so painful before – but not without (sacrifice of
joys?) once more throwing on this sinister line of effacement
the last lamented flowers once meant for him

[1] Oui Monsieur oui vous êtes mort
C'est ainsi du moins que votre lettre de faire-part
———

et rire au dedans de moi – affreux! en écrivant ceci est le
vôtre – vous qui verrez bien, ô mon – bien *[2]* aimé que si je
ne pouvais vous étreindre vous presser en mes bras – c'est
que vous étiez en moi
Cher compagnon des heures que je disais mauvaises, et non
moins plus tard de celles que plus tard je dis *[3]* meilleures
– comme s'il était encore – quel[s] qu'ils fussent, des
qualicatifs digne – etc. les heures où vous fûtes et ne fûtes
pas –

[1] moi – peut-être – l'ambiguité que cela se puisse!
[2] peine et jouissances douces du revenant malade

mère
il ne vivra pas! ———
deux –
père, devant tombeau (écarte mère? puis revient?
———

3ème partie

– père sacrificateur se dispose – mais idée (de lui) reste et
tout édifier là dessus – et offre à absolu?

Yes Sir yes you are dead
at least that is what your letter of announcement
——

and laughter inside me – hideous! in writing this is yours –
you who clearly will see O my – dearly beloved – that if I
could not embrace you squeeze you in my arms – it was
because you were in me
Dear companion of the hours which I used to call bad, and
no less so of those I later call better – as if he still was –
whichever they might have been, epithets worthy – etc. the
hours when you were and you were not –

me – perhaps – the ambiguity that it might be possible!
pain and sweet pleasures of the sick ghost

mother
he will not live! ——
two –
father, in front of tomb (moves mother aside? then comes
back?
——

3rd part

– sacrificing father readies himself – but idea (of him)
remains and build everything on this – then offer up to the
absolute?

2ème partie

amer
– ah! tant mieux que pas homme
mais ses yeux mais sa bouche
– qui parle ainsi? peut-être son amante. –
ô amante, fille que j'eusse aimée –
revenir à mère?

2ème partie

vu, revenu mort, à travers maladie – yeux, veulent bien
verser espoir.
– faire semblant consentir à jouer, avec indifférence –
il sait sans savoir et nous le pleurons sans le lui montrer
    assez de larmes – c'est introduire la mort –

1re partie

– on sent – coup fatal illuminant l'âme – que mort – et
(tonnerre) tout ce qui s'écroule –
rêve de lui laisser un nom, etc.

déjà si changé que ce n'est plus lui – et l'*idée* (de lui) *si!* ainsi
se dégage peu à peu.
——

plus tard, du moment que mort plane ——

2nd part

bitter
– Ah! just as well that not man
but his eyes but his mouth
– who speaks thus? perhaps his lover. –
O lover, girl I should have loved –
return to mother?

2nd part

seen, returned dead, through illness – eyes, would gladly
pour out hope.
– pretend to consent to play, with indifference –
he knows without knowing and we mourn him without
showing it
    enough tears – it is to let death in –

1st part

– we feel – fatal blow lighting up the soul – that death – and
(thunder) everything that tumbles down –
dream of leaving him a name, etc.

already so changed that it is no longer him – and thus the
idea (of him) *yes!* emerges little by little.
––––
later, from the moment death hovers ——

malade considéré comme mort
on aime déjà tel objet «qui le rappelle!»
ranger
———

et parfois espoir crève cette fiction de mort «non – il
vivra! –

vie réfugiée en nous ou la nôtre effroi – horreur de trou
s'attache ———
en faire le sacrifice –
– ou poèmes, pour plus tard, après nous, mort – être

que jamais yeux futurs, plein de terre ne se voilent de
temps ———

X

Je ne peux pas croire à tout ce qui s'est passé –
——— Le recom[m]encer en esprit au delà –
l'ensevelissement etc. –

sick considered dead
already we love this or that object 'which reminds us of him'
put away
——

and sometimes hope bursts this fiction of death 'no – he will
live! –

life taken shelter in us or ours dread – horror of hole clings
——

sacrifice him –
– or poems, for later, after us, death – being

that future eyes, filled with earth may never veil themselves
with time ——

X

I cannot believe in all that has happened –
—— To rebegin him in spirit beyond –
the burial etc. –

X

Mort!
Oh! tu crois que tu me le prendras ainsi – à cette mère – à
moi père
_____

j'avoue que tu peux beaucoup

[1]   X

que veux-tu, douce vision adorée – qui viens souvent vers
moi, te pencher – comme écouter secret (de mes larmes) –
savoir que tu es mort – ce que tu ignores? – non je ne [2] te
le dirai pas – car alors tu disparaîtrais – et je resterais seul
pleurant, toi, moi, mêlé, toi te pleurant enfant en moi
l'homme futur que tu ne seras pas, et qui reste sans vie ni
joie.

X

_____

vision sans cesse épurée par mes larmes

_____

X

Death!
Oh! you think you can take him away from me like this –
from this mother – from me father
———

I admit you can do much

X

what do you want, sweet loved vision – who often come
towards me, and lean over – as if listening to the secret (of
my tears) – know that you are dead – what you do not
know? – no I will not tell you – for then you would disappear
– and I would be alone weeping, for you, me, mingled, you
weeping for yourself child in me
the future man you will not become, and who am left
without life nor joy.

X

———

vision constantly purified by my tears
———

X

fin de I

Lui, mort – si beau, enfant
procédé – et que l'effroi farouche de mort tombe sur lui
(dérangé par cri de mère) avec l'homme qu'il eût dû être (vu
en cet instant suprême) pour rendre lit de mort

oh – pourvu qu'il n'en sache rien – ne se doute pas
_____

(pendant maladie
– mais d'où trahison

la mort ignorée –

X

non, je ne puis jeter terre de l'oubli
_____

(terre mère reprends le en ton ombre – et de même son esprit
en moi)
mère a saigné et pleuré
père sacrifie – et divinise

X

end of I

Him, dead – so beautiful, child
process – and that death's savage dread strikes him
(disturbed by mother's cry) with the man he should have
been (seen in this supreme instant) to render death bed

oh – provided he knows nothing of it – does not suspect
___

(during sickness
– but whence betrayal

death unknown –

X

no, I cannot throw earth of forgetting
___

(earth mother take him back into your shadow – and also
his spirit in me)
mother bled and wept
father sacrifices – and deifies

II

pas moi – en moi –

———

et absence –

———

oppos. IV ou IV
le toujours soi, rien que soi! torturant l'âme délicate qu'on
aime –

[1]   X

sous entendre peut-être la cérémonie – pompes funèbres
etc. – bref ce qu'a vu le monde – (enterrement messe? pour
ramener [2] cela à l'intimité – la chambre – vide – absence –
ouverte – le moment où son absence finit pour qu'il soit en
nous –
– ce serait cette 3ᵉ partie – [3] après qu'il a été enlevé parti
de la chambre –
– voir alors comment II – «la maladie et le petit fantôme» –
s'encadreraient –
– III revenant [4] par dessus, vers la fin de II – mort – ainsi
meubles immortalité
et fond de nature
I – il ne jouera plus – se mêlant à campagne où il repose?

particulariser?   X

Ah! cœur adorable
ô mon image là bas des trop grands destins – qu'enfant
comme toi – je rêve encore tout seul – en l'avenir –

60

II

not me – in me –

––––

and absence –

––––

oppos. IV or IV
the perpetual self, just the self – torturing the delicate soul
we love –

X

perhaps imply the ceremony – funeral etc. – in short what
the world saw – (burial mass? to bring it all back to intimacy
– the room – empty – absence – open – the moment when
his absence ends, so he can be in us –
– that would be this 3rd part – after he has been taken away,
left the room –
– then see how II – 'the sickness and the little ghost' – would
be framed –
– III returning over, towards end of II – death – thus
furniture immortality
and background of nature
I – he will no longer play – mingling with the countryside
he rests in?

particularise?   X

Ah! adorable heart
O my image of destinies too great beyond – that as child like
you – I still dream alone – in the future –

[ff⁰ˢ 164, 165]

[1]   X

Oh! tu sais bien que si je consens à vivre – à paraître t'oublier
– c'est pour nourrir ma douleur – et que cet oubli apparent
jaillisse plus vif en larmes, à [2] un moment quelconque, au
milieu de cette vie, quand tu m'y apparais

[ff⁰ˢ 166, 167, 168]

[1]   X

temps – que corps met à s'oblitérer en terre – (se confondre
peu à peu avec terre neutre aux vastes horizons)
c'est alors qu'il lâche l'esprit pur que l'on [2] fut – et qui etait
lié à lui, organisé – lequel peut, pur se réfugier en nous,
régner en nous, survivants – (ou en [3] la pureté absolue, sur
laquelle le temps pivote et se refait – (jadis *Dieu*) état le plus
divin ——

[f⁰ 169]

        X

moi qui le sais pour lui porte un terrible secret!
père – lui, trop enfant pour de telles choses
———
je le sais, c'est en cela que *son être* est perpétué –

[f⁰ 170]

je le sens en moi qui *veut* – sinon la vie perdue, du moins
l'équivalent –
la mort – où l'on est dépouillé de corps – en ceux qui restent

X

Oh! you know that if I consent to live – to seem to forget you – it is to feed my pain – and so that this seeming forgetting may spring forth more painfully in tears, at a given moment, in the midst of this life, when you appear to me in it

X

time – that body takes to obliterate itself in earth – (to merge little by little with neutral earth on the vast horizons) it is then that he lets go of the pure spirit which we were – and which was bound up with him, organised – which can, pure take refuge in us, reign in us, survivors (or in absolute purity, on which time pivots and remakes itself – (formerly *God*) the most divine state ——

X

I who know it for him carry a dreadful secret! father – he, too much a child for such things
———
I *know* it, this is how *his being* is perpetuated –

I can feel him in me *wanting* – if not lost life, at least the equivalent –
death – where we are stripped of body – in those who remain

[1]   X

et alors III
lui parler ainsi
Ami, n'est-ce pas que tu triomphes n'est-ce pas dégagé de
tout poids de la vie – du vieux mal de vivre (oh! je *[2]* te sens
bien fort – et que tu te trouves bien toujours avec nous, père,
mère, – mais libre, enfant éternel, et partout à la fois –
——

et les dessous – je peux *[3]* dire cela parce que je garde toute
ma douleur pour nous –
– la douleur de ne pas être – que tu ignores – et que je
m'impose (cloîtré, du reste, hors de la *[4]* vie où tu me mènes
(ayant ouvert pour nous un monde de mort ——

[1]   X

l'ensevelissement moral
– père mère
Oh ne le cache pas encore etc. –
amie la terre attend – l'acte pieux, de la cacher
– laisse *[2]* l'autre mère – commune de tous les hommes –
(dans laquelle va le lit – où il est maintenant) le prendre –
laisse les hommes apparus – oh! les *[3]* les hommes – ces
hommes (croque mort – ou amis?) l'emporter suivi de
larmes – etc. – vers terre mère à tous *[4]* mère à tous – la
sienne maintenant et (puisqu'elle participe déjà de *toi*, ta
fosse creusée par lui? –) lui devenu petit homme – visage
grave d'homme ——

X

and so III
speak to him like this
Friend, you triumph do you not free from all of life's weight
– from the old sickness of living (oh! I feel you so strongly)
and that you are certainly always with us, father, mother, –
but free, eternal child, and everywhere at once –
——

and the losses – I can say this because I am keeping all my
pain for us –
– the pain of not being – which you know nothing of – and
which I take upon myself (cloistered, moreover, away from
the life to which you bring me (having opened for us a world
of death) ——

X

the spiritual burial
– father mother
Oh do not hide him yet, etc. –
friendly earth wait – the holy act, of hiding him
– let the other mother – common to all men – (into which
goes the bed – where he is now) take him – let the men who
have appeared – oh! the men – these men (undertakers – or
friends?) carry him off followed by tears – etc. – towards
earth mother of all mother of all – his now and (since she is
already part of *you*, your tomb dug by him?–) he become
little man – sombre man's face ——

X

complices de mort
c'est pendant maladie – moi pensant mère – ? et sachant

fermer les yeux – je ne veux pas fermer les yeux –
– qui me regarderont toujours –

────

ou *mort à part* yeux fermés, etc.
on le revoit en madadie luttant contre ce état gisant –

X

petit corps qui un instant avant était lui mis de côté par mort
une main
– et cri, sans presque faire attention à ce corps mis à part –
O mon fils comme vers un ciel instinct spiritualiste

X

suspens – rupture – partie –
Oh! ce sacrifice – pour cela nier sa vie – pour l'ensevelir –
causons de lui encore, évoquons – en réalité, silence

X

death's accomplices
it is during the sickness – me thinking mother – ? and
knowing

close the eyes – I do not want to close the eyes –
– that will look at me forever –
‾‾‾
or *death aside* eyes closed, etc.
we see him again in sickness fighting against this state –

X

little body which a moment before was him put aside by
death a hand
– and cry, almost without paying attention to this body put
aside –
O my son as towards a heaven spiritualist instinct

X

suspension – rupture – part –
Oh! this sacrifice – for this to deny his life – to bury him –
let us talk about him some more, let us evoke – in reality,
silence

[1]   X

rupture | en deux
j'écris – lui (sous terre) décomposition
mère voit – ce qu'elle devrait ignorer ——
puis maladie il revient jusqu'a ce que, tout épuré! (par mal)
et couché – si beau mort – que fiction tombeau (on le fait
disparaître – pour qu'il reste en [2] nous
son *regard* (conscience) – longtemps regardé pendant
maladie
——

ou alors triomphe après –
3ᵉ partie
rupture entre I et II et entre II et III
tout se rattache –

        X

ne pas savoir son bonheur quand il *est* là – … trouvé cela si
naturel ——
relier à l'inconscience de mort –
——

        X

vrai deuil en l'appartement – meubles – pas cimetière –

X

rupture | in two
I write – him (under ground) decomposition
mother sees – what she was meant not to know ——
then sickness he returns until, wholly purified! (by disease)
and lying down – so beautiful dead – tomb but fiction (we
make it disappear – so that he remains in us
his *look* (consciousness) – long watched through illness

——

or then triumph after –
3rd part
rupture between I and II and between II and III
everything connects –

X

not to know his happiness when he *is* there – ... found that
so natural ——
link back to unconsciousness of death –

——

X

true bereavement in the apartment – furniture – not
cemetery –

X

trouver *absence seule* –
– en présence de petits vêtements – etc. – mère.

X

petit marin – costume mis
quoi! – pour grande traversée
une vague t'emporta
mer ascite

[1]   X

fiction de l'absence gardée par mère – appartement
«je ne sais pas ce qu'ils en ont fait – dans le trouble et les
pleurs d'alors – je sais seule[2]ment qu'il n'est plus ici et si,
il y est – absent – d'où mère elle-même fantôme devenue –
spiritualisée par habitude de vivre avec une vision
[3] tandis que lui père – qui construisit le tombeau – mura
… sait – et son esprit n'y va-t-il pas chercher les traces de
destruction – et transmuer en esprit pur? [4] si bien que la
pureté sort de la corruption!
———
mais M – a suivi au cimetière.

X

to find *absence only* –
– in presence of little clothes – etc. – mother.

X

little sailor – sailor suit
what! – for great crossing
a wave carried you away
sea ascites

X

fiction of absence kept by mother – apartment
'I do not know what they have done with him – amid the
worry and the tears at the time – I know only that he is no
longer here and yes, he is here – absent – whence mother
herself become a ghost – spiritualised from habit of living
with a vision
whereas he father – who built the tomb – walled in … knows
– and does his spirit not go there searching for the traces of
destruction – and transmute into pure spirit? so that purity
emerges from corruption!
——
but M – followed in the cemetery.

non – je ne laisserai pas le néant ——
Père – je sens le néant m'envahir

X

et si au moins – esprit – je n'ai pas donné sang suffisant –
– que ma pensée lui fasse une vie plus belle plus pure.
——
– et comme sa peur de moi – qui pense – à côté de lui –

Quoi, ce que je dis est vrai – ce n'est pas seulement musique
– etc.

bouquets
on se sent obligé de jeter en cette terre qui s'ouvre devant
l'enfant – les plus beaux bouquets – les plus beaux produits,
de cette terre – sacrifiés – pour voiler [2] (ou lui faire payer
son forfait –
——

72

no – I will not let nothingness ——
Father – I feel the nothingness invade me

      X

and if at least – spirit – I have not given adequate blood –
– let my thought make him a purer more beautiful life.
——

– and like his fear of me – who thinks – beside him –

What, what I am saying is true – it is not only music – etc.

flowers
we feel obliged to throw into this earth that opens before the
child – the most beautiful flowers – the most beautiful
offerings, of this earth – sacrificed – to veil (or make him pay
his forfeit –
——

[1]   II

lutte des deux père et fils l'un pour conserver fils en pensée
– idéal – l'autre pour vivre, se relevant etc. –
– interruptions carence) –
[2] ainsi
et mère soigne le bien – soins de mère interrompant pensée
– et enfant entre père qui le pense mort, et mère
vie –
– «soigne le bien etc.
– d'où
[3] Ce n'est qu'en III qu'*éclat* de ceci (brisure) causé par cri
de I – se raccorde peu à peu – tout fini

          (fin
enfant
destinée
terre le dit consolante –

Le père *grave*
c'est à moi qu'il appartient ayant donné l'être de ne pas le
laisser perdre –trouble
et mère – je ne veux pas qu'il cesse (*idée* là!)

II

struggle of the two father and son the one to preserve son
in thought – ideal – the other to live, rising up etc. –
– interruptions lack) –
so
and mother tend him well – mother's cares interrupting
thought – and child between father who thinks him dead,
and mother
life –
– 'tend him well etc.
– whence
Only in III does the *explosion* of this (rupture) caused by cry
of I – connect back together little by little – all finished

      (end
child
destiny
earth calls it consolatory –

The *solemn* father
it is up to me having given him life not to let him be taken
– worry
and mother – I do not want him to stop being (*idea* there!)

(1
apparue!
– ombre du jour pauvre et dont je ne me doutais pas
malheur
mère et fils jusqu'au port

(2
si ce n'est châtiment
les enfants des autres classes

─────

alors que furieuse contre tous
société vile qui devait l'écraser peut-être

par la guerre d'un mal me rattrape à cela
prêtre

(1
appeared!
– shadow of the wretched day and of which I had no
suspicion
disaster
mother and son to the port

2)
unless it is punishment
children of other classes
——

whereas furious with everyone
vile society that would have crushed him perhaps

by the war of one sickness redeem myself by that
priest

l'enfant supprimé
– l'amour n'est
qu'un vœu d'enfant
      infinité
sans l'enfant nul
élan assez vaste –
      vers quoi
car c'est vers un
corps-de-Soi

l'enfant qui sera
soi – famille –
et semeur à son
         tour

the lost child
– love is
only a child's wish
      infinity
without the child no
flight vast enough –
      towards which
for it is towards a
body-of-Self

the child who will be
self – family –
and sower in his
        turn

AFTERWORD

Mallarmé and the *Tombeau d'Anatole*

While there are no references to a *tombeau* poem for Anatole in Mallarmé's multi-volume *Correspondance*, one of several posthumous references to Anatole occurs in a letter to Jeanne Michaud, a year after the boy's death, in which Mallarmé writes about the anniversary of the death as being another – and final – phase of the child's removal:

> This anniversary day is very painful for us, not because it brings our thoughts back to where they are, of their own accord, all day long; but because it closes the cycle of time when we could say to ourselves 'Our darling child was still alive, doing this or that, a year ago...'. This period has now come full circle and – alas! – we feel further from him now, his lovely precious life. A new separation.[1]

Calendar time has helped cushion the family from loss, not by creating distance between them and the event, but by keeping the dead child close. The anniversary, is a 'new separation', closing the cycle of measured and measurable time – hours, instants, a year – that allow the bereaved to revisit in the loop of memory the altogether less measurable piece of time that is a life.

Another anniversary and another death which bear comparison with Anatole's are fictional ones in a story from *Cruel Tales* by Mallarmé's friend Villiers de l'Isle-Adam. The story is called 'Véra', and was first published in 1874. In Villiers's tale, a young aristocrat, the Count of Athol, knows that the death of his young wife Véra need not present any insuperable difficulty to their life together. Having entombed her, in the course of what is called a 'dreadful ceremony', the young Count returns to their house to find the evidence of her life all around him: her dress, thrown off the night before, spread out on the armchair; her jewellery;

81

her half-open fan lying on the chimney; an open grand piano evoking 'a forever unfinished melody'.[2] That 'forever unfinished' is the key – both final and incomplete. The imprint of her head is still on the pillow: the world, their world, is still moulded to her shape. Confronting the world of her objects, a world where her *things* attest to her having been – as if they themselves weren't aware that she had gone – the Count finds that the real cemetery is the house, something Mallarmé discovers when he returns from Anatole's funeral:

> true bereavement in the apartment – furniture – not cemetery –

One of Mallarmé's many struggles in his projected poem is with the world of things, of matter – the boy's clothes, his room, his bed, toys left in mid-play, the flat. The child's games too are 'forever unfinished', and in one of the sheets for the *tombeau*, the moment the child stops playing is invested with special poetic significance. The funeral ceremony is an ordeal: the horrible physicality of the little body in the coffin, the earth thrown over it, the undertakers ('croque-morts' is the brutal French term Mallarmé uses), the procession, and the return home to a different kind of cemetery, one in which the child is not in fact 'buried' but constantly referred to. However, in Mallarmé's empty flat, it is Anatole's *absence* that is called up – in the Count of Athol's house, it is Véra's *presence*. This is how Mallarmé describes the funeral ceremony:

> moment when we must break with the living memory, to bury him – put him in the coffin, hide him – with the brutalities of
> the laying in the coffin rough contact etc.

In Villiers's 'Véra', the young Count takes his cue from the interrupted objects which belonged to his wife, resolving to go on living exactly as if she hadn't died. He orders his manservant to continue serving them both meals, and for a year he reads her poetry, talks to her, makes tea for two in the garden, chats to her as she sits, in his mind's eye, in her usual armchair. His servant, initially thinking his master insane, gradually begins not only to grow used to the apparent fiction, but to participate in it, so much so that after a while he has to keep reminding himself that she is '*positively* dead':

> [Raymond] saw that sooner or later he would give in completely to the terrifying magnetism with which the Count penetrated the atmosphere around them.[3]

This 'magnetism', the Count's refusal to believe, and to believe in, what has happened, gradually draws Véra back into the world of the living. After a time, the most extraordinary things begin to happen: he hears her, she brushes past him, her perfume riding the air in her invisible wake. He can smell her sleeping beside him. Even Raymond begins to see the swish of her dress on the stairwell, hears her voice calling him from the living room, and sees these phenomena as perfectly normal occurrences. '[S]he *thinks* she is dead', says Athol, turning the tables on death, so that being dead, rather than still alive, is the illusory, misplaced faith, the fiction belied by reality.

On the anniversary of her death, Athol finds her jewellery still warm from her wrists and neck: 'the exquisite magnetism of the beautiful dead woman still penetrated the jewellery'. The magnetism – a force which Villiers borrows from science to describe the power of the imagination over the world of things – has brought Véra back. A year after her death, she returns:

> And there, before his eyes, made up of will and memory, leaning on her elbows, fluid on the lace pillow, her hands holding her heavy black hair, mouth half-open and with a smile emparadised [*emparadisé*] with voluptuousness, beautiful to die for in fact! the Countess Véra was watching him, still a little sleepy.[4]

In this marvellous and exultant passage, replete with grave-straddling puns ('belle à en mourir', goes the French), Véra returns to a world which would not let her go, which was never convinced that she had gone in the first place. The alliance of the transforming imagination of an individual with a houseful of inanimate but animated objects has pulled Véra back from the other side.

In Villiers's story, the Count, the house and Véra's things invite her to go on living; they *demand* it. They constantly call her up, not just to memory, but to the world she has just left, as a magnet calls up iron filings. They do so by flatly denying death, by not even referring to it, except as a fiction, a fallacy. In the *Tombeau d'Anatole*, however, Mallarmé, the bereaved father, looks at the boy's things – his clothes especially – only to find, as he says, nothing:

to find *absence only* –
– in presence of little clothes – etc. – mother.
[…]
little sailor – sailor suit
what! – for great crossing
a wave carried you away
sea ascites

In the original French, the word 'mère' for mother evokes by association the word 'mer' for sea. Anatole was buried in his sailor suit, and the 'wave' that carries him away is mentioned here alongside the only reference to the illness from which he died: ascites. One of the Mallarméan themes this fragment calls poignantly to mind is the loving descriptions of clothes that occur in *La Dernière Mode*, the fashion journal Mallarmé had been editing a few years before: evocative and graceful clothes for boys and girls aged seven to ten years.

In Villiers's story, however, Athol makes a vulgar blunder: at the moment of kissing Véra, he suddenly remembers that she is in fact dead: 'Now I remember! […] but you're dead'. Véra disappears at once, and the fiction that had kept reality at bay collapses. At this moment, the objects in the house lose their faith: 'The *Certainty* of all the objects suddenly disappeared'. Now, a full year after dying,

Véra is dead. The anniversary has culminated both in Véra's return and in her final dispersal. If Mallarmé cannot believe that his son has died, Anatole's clothes do not, unlike Véra's, *believe* that he has not. In one of the sheets for the poem Mallarmé writes, echoing the end of 'Véra': 'no I will not tell you – for then you would disappear'. The father looks to these clothes, only to find they have no *certitude*. The journey of the 'little sailor' is one which links the poem with Mallarmé's many poetic seafaring adventures from 'Salut' to *A Throw of the Dice*. In fact the reflex – understandable in any bereavement – to move away from the empty clothes to the consolatory abstraction of an imagined journey brings in a further reflex on Mallarmé's part: to steer Anatole's death into the gentler current of one of his own more familiar poetic themes: the sea journey.

Sheet 150 (p. 55) of Mallarmé's manuscript reads as follows:

> I cannot believe in all that has happened –
> —— To rebegin him in spirit beyond –
> the burial etc. –

There are two contradictory impulses struggling here: on the one hand, the father refusing to believe, in the sense of believing *in*, what has happened (that Anatole has died); on the other, an attempt to *rebegin* Anatole beyond ('au delà'), for which he as poet knows he *must* believe in what has happened, in order to undertake the child's continuation. This too is part of a drama, often figured as a struggle *with* the child, that dominates the attempted poem. The boy fights against death, wants to live an earthly life, while the poet, designing the tomb, is complicit with death by trying to ensure him an afterlife. Some of the most moving passages in the notes describe the boy sitting up and refusing to die, interrupting the father's tomb-building, and resisting the processes of resurrection, absorption and continuation for which he is being primed.

The reason for comparing Villiers's fantastical story and Mallarmé's poem around the painful reality of the death of his son is to show up two radically different, but comparable, versions of death, and their treatment by the creative imagination. In each case, this imagination is confronted with a similar set of circumstances, but reacts in markedly different ways. In Villiers, resisting and reversing death means denying death; in the Mallarmé poem we find the poet accepting death in order to build the death-resistant memorial poem. There is another Mallarmé poem which seems to replay these themes and which is held to have been influenced by Villiers's *Véra*. It is a poem of 1877: 'Pour votre chère morte, son ami'. The two final stanzas go as follows:

> Qui veut souvent avoir la Visite ne doit
> Par trop de fleurs charger la pierre que mon doigt
> Soulève avec l'ennui d'une force défunte.
>
> Âme au si clair foyer tremblante de m'asseoir,
> Pour revivre il suffit qu'à tes lèvres j'emprunte
> Le souffle de mon nom murmuré tout un soir.[5]

Who wishes to be visited must not / With too many flowers weigh down the stone which my finger / Lifts with the idleness of a dead strength.

Soul of such bright homestead trembling to sit / To live again I need only borrow from your lips / The breath of my name murmured all evening long.

In this poem, the dead woman tells her beloved not to accept her death, not to load the tomb down with flowers or she will never be able to climb out of it. The weight of flowers, a weight which turns up several times in Mallarmé's notes for Anatole's *tombeau*, is here a metaphor for the idea that the living, by believing that the dead one has in fact died, are actually largely *responsible* for making death irrevocable. The tombstone is weightless and easily lifted; the flowers, token of the lover's belief in death *as a fact*, constitute the real unmovable weight. As Paul Celan writes in *Backlight*:

'So strong was his love for her it would have pushed open the lid of his coffin – had the flower she placed on it not been so heavy'.[6] In Mallarmé, as in Celan, it is not death itself but the living's acceptance of death that closes the tomb.

Mallarmé frequently refers to the actual burial, often in terms of the 'contact' between body and coffin, between body and earth, at one point even referring to the 'décomposition' of the body. At one stage in the draft of this poem he plans to 'imply' ('sous-entendre') the ceremony:

perhaps imply the ceremony – funeral etc. – in short what the world saw – (burial mass? to bring it all back to intimacy – the room – empty – absence – open – the moment when his absence ends, so he can be in us –
– that would be this 3rd part – after he has been taken away, left the room –
– then see how II – 'the sickness and the little ghost' – would be framed –
– III returning over, towards end of II – death – thus furniture immortality
and background of nature
I – he will no longer play – mingling with the countryside he rests in?

In common with many of his poems, Mallarmé reverts to the empty room, the nothingness in and upon which it is possible to dream a *something*. If the cemetery, the coffin, the earth and the gravediggers, and all the brute trappings of a 'laying in the coffin' are the intractable realities which refuse to bend to the imaginative will of the poet, then the empty room is altogether more familiar territory, like the sea which is evoked in the empty sailor suit. Both are passages not just from the concrete to the abstract and back, but from an unbendable reality to a more malleable basis for poetic fiction. This reversion to a productive absence, a fertile emptiness, is also another specifically Mallarméan poetic reflex coming to the aid of the normal reflexes of bereavement. Mallarmé tries to enfold Anatole's death into the familiar system not just of poetry but of his own poetry.

If we read these two examples – the sea journey and the attempt to 'bring back' the poem to empty open room – as Mallarmé's attempts to guide the reality into his own poetic and imaginative idiom, then we can get a better idea of just what he's up against, and of what it is in the notes for the poem that might have made it impossible to finish.

It was W.B. Yeats who compared finishing a poem with shutting a box; Mallarmé, by that token, may have found, as he contemplated similar images throughout these notes, that shutting the lid, sealing the coffin, placing the 'heavy headstone' on this *tombeau* were altogether harder to achieve. In one sheet, Mallarmé further immaterialises the ceremony, choosing as his model a pagan ceremony dedicated to preservation of the body:

> ancient egypt – embalment – days, operations, crypts – all this change, once barbaric and external – material – now spiritual and in us

This is not just a *tombeau*, then, but a kind of perpetuation. This internal – 'spiritual and in us' – embalment, is something Mallarmé begins not with the dead body but with the living one. Here again we note a movement away from external or concrete things into their abstract equivalents in the world of wishful imagination. The poet starts to do this not *after* the death, but before it: it is a pre-emptive embalment, which both son and mother refuse to join.

His plans for the poem suggest something along the following lines: first Anatole is struck down, not dead but 'stricken to death', a distinction important to Mallarmé, who on 22 August 1879 writes a letter to Henry Roujon:

> I hardly dare to give you any news because there are moments in this combat between life and death going on in our darling child when I have hope, and repent for a pessimistic letter I have just written, like some messenger of ill-luck I have myself sent.

This is a quite natural fear of causing, by imagining, the

worst, all perfectly comprehensible in the circumstances; indeed, *For Anatole's Tomb* is a moving account, however fractured, of the consolations and inconsolability of bereavement. Here too, however, the poet is disturbed by the notion – here figured as an ordinary superstition – that speculating on the future might be, possibly, also to shape it. Yet the notes describe a process that seems to do exactly what Mallarmé in the Roujon letter is avoiding: imagining the worst before it has happened. Part I of the poem was to end when the mother cries out in pain and dread at Anatole's first convulsion and loss of consciousness: 'He is dead!' The space between the wife's cry and the child's death becomes the poem's space, the designated site of the *tombeau*. And yet, we note, it is the mother who enunciates the worst, not the father, as if she were committing the predictive indecency Mallarmé describes to Roujon. We further notice that the mother goes back on her utterance, tries to cancel out what she has said, as if she had pronounced, only to retract, a death sentence. But in the silent, thinking father, the idea takes root and becomes the *Tomb*, imagined and erected around the still-living child, growing up around its incumbent.

'He is dead!', is the mother's cry at the close of Part I. The end of this phase of the poem ushers in, as a theme, the settlement of the illness which is to be the second part of the poem, but in which Mallarmé already sees the child as dead. In the poem itself, the biological death was to come in Part III, linked to Part I by the continuation of the same cry, intermitted, by an illness which is not so much a curable sickness as a slow-motion development towards death. In Part II, the sick Anatole is already a 'ghost' (the French 'revenant' emphasises the idea of return) from beyond the grave, from a 'death' which Mallarmé thinks about 'implying' rather than stating. Instead of the mind adjusting to a fact in aftermath, the fact of death comes as an aftermath to the mind's realisation.

Mallarmé writes at one point of the 'poetry of sickness', and sickness plays an ambiguous role in this poetic endeavour: on the one hand, it wards off death; on the other it kills. For the poet, for whom the real biological death is not the spur to the poem's conception but the culmination in reality of a process undertaken in the imagination, the sickness is an essential player in the drama. Sickness is the ally of poetry, because, at once deadly and death-defying, it provides the writing space. In the projected structure of this *tombeau* we have the following: the death that *is* mentioned (by the mother in Part I) is not in fact death; the one that Mallarmé decides not to mention (but instead to imply) in Part III is the real one. The ceremony, the mourning, the cortège: all these are figured not as concrete events but as objectifications of thought processes in the poet's mind. Above the illness, linking a still-living Anatole with a dead Anatole, hovers one cry, the mother's 'Il est mort!', which she refuses to believe, but from which the father *as poet* dates the death.

> end of I
> – O terror he is dead! –
> – he *is* ... dead (absolutely – i.e. stricken
> so mother sees him
> in such a way that, sick, he seems to come back – or to see
> himself again in the future – obtained in the present
>
> mother I
> no one can die with such eyes, etc. –
> father lets out in his terror, sobs 'he is dead'
> – and it is in the wake of that cry, that II the child sits up
> in his bed – looks around, etc –
> and III perhaps nothing – about death and simply
> implied
> – in the space of 'he is dead of I II
> ⎯⎯⎯

The illness collapses time frames, by allowing the child to travel ahead first to what he would have been, and then back to the present with the image of the 'race' to come. In his liminal and extreme state, he is already a ghost, a returner from beyond, travelling back and forth along the illness that both kills and has already killed him, but which also keeps him alive. The moment of death is 'implied' from the status given – poetically and structurally – to a false alarm uttered by the mother and shaped by the father into a prediction. But the boy is not willing to submit: 'he gets up in his bed, searches'. This is one of two occasions in the notes for the poem on which he seems to rise up during – and also against – processes which are taking their course first on his body – illness, death – and secondly on his memory – his father's *tombeau* poem, before he has even died.

From the start then, and integral to the planning of the poem, the poet's imaginative processes, which in for example 'Véra' or 'Pour votre chère morte' might have kept Anatole alive, are in fact preparing his tomb. Alive and ill, the boy is being embalmed. Mallarmé's many references to the practical 'cares' of the mother, tending to the living body, are opposed to the internal, 'spiritual and in us' embalming carried out by the poet/father at the same time. The opposition between what the mother does – tending to the physical – and what the poet/father does as he tends to the abstract and internal – refining the physical away – is a source of conflict.

On sheets 198–202 (p. 75), we see this played out, in what Mallarmé clearly sees as a struggle between father and son, one fighting for life, the other fighting for afterlife. Part II will contain:

> II
>
> struggle of the two father and son the one to preserve son in thought – ideal – the other to live, rising up etc. –
> – interruptions lack) –
> so
> and mother tend him well – mother's cares interrupting thought – and child between father who thinks him dead, and mother
> life –

– 'tend him well etc.
– whence
Only in III does the *explosion* of this (rupture) caused by
cry of I – connects back together little by little – all
finished

   (end
child
destiny
earth calls it consolatory –

The *solemn* father
it is up to me having given him life not to let him be taken
– worry
and mother – I do not want him to stop being (*idea* there!)

In the previous quotation Anatole 'gets up'; in this one he
is 'rising up'. The image of the child 'rising' calls up
precisely the wrong form of resurrection, because it is the
raising up of the living body refusing to die, rather than the
spirit disengaging from the dead body. The word 'thought'
is highly charged here, repeated, as often in the poem, to
divide father and mother. In sheet 134 (p. 49) we have the
brutal:

to mother
you cry – me, I'm thinking

'Preserve the child in thought': to preserve the son in an
afterlife; then the 'mother's cares', presumably tending to
the body in this life, interrupting the 'thought'; then the
father 'who thinks him dead' – who thinks him to be dead,
but also actively thinks him dead, thinks him *to death*. In 180
(p. 67) he sees the boy struggling, this time against the
sickness to which, as Mallarmé writes, the parents cling in
order to keep the child longer. In the previous sheet we have
this near admission of a parental conspiracy:

death's accomplices
it is during the sickness – me thinking mother – ? and
knowing

Four consecutive sheets, essential to the drama, go as follows:

> The sacrifice – on the tomb
> purple king, mother love
> it is necessary – so he can be again – ! (transfusion) mother
> wants to have him herself, she is earth –
>
> > Since it *has to be*
> > What are you saying there –
> don't interrupt me –
>
> > I
>
> mother's fears – he stopped playing today
> father listens – sees mother's eyes – lets her tend to II
> he is thinking –
>
> > II
>
> mother's tears
> room
> calming down little by little in the double perspective
> child, destiny –
> tomb, memory old man –
> – (who is speaking)   [96–9 (pp. 33–5)]

The poet who is trying urgently to remove the 'material side' from the process finds that the boy's mother and mother earth are in league against him. The poet/father merges two rivals into one, with the result that the potentially comforting notion of the earth reclaiming its own in a gentle rite of physical reabsorption is jeopardised by an image of marital struggle. Time and again in these notes a consolatory movement, something that might make sense of or give sense to all this grief and loss, is blocked.

A further conflict between father and mother is brought out when she follows the Count of Athol by refusing to accept the child's death, despite having been at the funeral:

fiction of absence kept by mother – apartment
'I do not know what they have done with him – amid the
worry and the tears at the time – I know only that he is
no longer here and yes, he is here – absent – whence
mother herself has become a ghost – spiritualised by
habit of living with a vision
whereas he father – who built the tomb – walled in …
knows – and does his spirit not go there searching for the
traces of destruction – and transmute into pure spirit? so
that purity emerges from corruption!
___
but M – followed in the cemetery.

Here the tomb's designer, the father who 'walled in' the son
in advance of his death, confronts the mother who, even
faced with the brutal fact of having followed in the
cemetery, refuses to believe in what has happened. The
poem cannot propose a solution to this opposition. Indeed,
the cemetery scene might have been a scene of unbridgeable
conflict: one sheet has the lines 'father, in front of tomb
(moves mother aside? then comes back?', and although the
image is of 'sparing' her the grief, which would be the
altruistic *motive*, the sustained *motif* is of the boy's second
birth into the father's mind, which would be its opposite:
the sidelining of the mother, here pushed to the margins of
her own grief. The mother thinks him alive when he's dead,
the poet/father thinks him dead while he's still alive. The
tombeau-writer meets extraordinary resistance, against
which both his ordinary consolation and his grand
metaphysical schemes for 'reabsorption', 'resurrection',
'continuation' are powerless. This death, like most real
things, and certainly like all real deaths, tests these
metaphysical schemes to their limit.

There is a sense in these notes of the poetic imagination
constantly uncovering its reflexes and motivations and not
finding them innocent or blameless enough to see the poem
through to the end. The poetic and the imaginative have
been working with death rather than resisting it. 'Guilt' has

been mentioned, but guilt at what, and how is the guilt figured? One way in which it finds expression is in the notion of heredity, of having handed on 'bad blood' to the son. On sheets 118–19 (p. 43) 'the father cursing his blood' faces the question;

> What! was he then born not to be
> mother he was too beautiful too
> and terror in father cursing his blood
> – the mother – yes, made for being, his eyes – what good so
> much spirit etc. – he will live! (last cry) treatments, etc.
> death at least take him without his knowing
> or mother (sometimes, he turns away from me, and such
> terrible sacrifice
> – father will redeem everything later by prolonging his
> being, reabsorbing etc.

These references to the 'hereditary' nature of Anatole's illness on the one hand blame the father, on the other absolve him as helpless fellow-victim. Moreover, in the model of genetic short-circuiting that heredity offers, father and son become one. Hereditary illness has one necessary facet in the status given it in the poem: it dooms Anatole, by being there, inside him, as part of him – an illness from within and not from without. It is this, perhaps more than death itself, and certainly more than a caught illness, that kills him. For the poet who attempts to 'imply' death, it is also one way of implying the possible guilt he might feel at having 'doomed' Anatole by setting to work on his *tombeau* while he was still alive, at thinking him dead in advance. A fateful heredity becomes perhaps a way of insinuating a misused imagination that has set about building a tomb for the living. Perhaps Mallarmé's need to blame his 'bad blood' is a means of implying the blame he attaches to himself for having started to write, and for all the 'thinkings' and the 'knowings' that pit him against his wife, his child and himself. 'Heredity' might be dreadful to countenance, but at least, even in its brutality, it explains – something the poem is at a loss to do – and it explains by apportioning responsibility but not blame. When we see that Mallarmé explores the notion that Anatole too was going to be a poet, to carry on his work, then the business of writing poetry joins up with the 'bad blood': both are 'handed down'. One is a vocation, the other is a sickness, and both meet up in the notion of 'poetry of sickness' – perhaps with a ghostly inversion to 'sickness of poetry'.

This poem was to have been both the child's *tombeau* and his 'continuation', a laying to rest and a site of rebirth. One word which translation cannot convey the duality of, and which recurs throughout Mallarmé's notes, is the word 'encore'. Meaning either 'again' or 'still', the French holds both senses in a way that a translator – forced to choose between them – cannot convey. Mallarmé also uses words like 'reabsorption', 'continuation', 'transfusion' in an attempt to write Anatole's death as what he calls in one sheet a 'change of mode of being'. Anatole's death was to have been the crossing of what Mallarmé described in his *tombeau* of Verlaine, the 'shallow stream' ('peu profond ruisseau') of death. To judge from these notes the poem would have sought to bridge different states of being, and to chart the crossing of the river Styx diminished by a poet's transforming imagination into little more than a shallow stream. Structurally too, as we have seen, the constituent sections of the poem would have been connected by chronological arches, bridges across past and present, but also across generations and epochs. More ambitiously even, it would have connected the world of spirit with the world of matter. Yet this proved impossible for Mallarmé to write, partly perhaps because, ranged against the vocabulary of continuity, resolution and restitution, there is the insistence of words denoting rupture, crisis, and loss. For every projected cohesion – between life and death, father and son, mother and father, past and present, matter and spirit – there is also a terminal chasm which cannot be imagined away.

Perhaps because of its extraordinary ambition of poetic and philosophical scope, the text of this poem seems at once a foundation and a ruin; depending on whether one reads it backwards or forwards, *For Anatole's Tomb* can appear a site in perpetual mid-construction, or the debris of something that once was, now derelict and overgrown. Like the *tombeau* it wanted to be, it is a project that both abolishes itself and promises its own future resurrection.

Notes

1 Mallarmé, *Correspondance*, II, ed. Henri Mondor and Lloyd James Austin (Paris: Gallimard, 1965) pp. 212–13. For a selection of Mallarmé's letters in English translation, see *Selected Letters of Stéphane Mallarmé*, ed. and trans. Rosemary Lloyd (Chicago: University of Chicago Press, 1988).
2 Villiers de l'Isle-Adam, *Œuvres complètes*, 2 vols, ed. Alan Raitt and Pierre-Georges Castex (Paris: Pléiade, 1986); I, p. 554.
3 Ibid., p. 557.
4 Ibid., p. 560.
5 Mallarmé, *Œuvres complètes*, ed. Bertrand Marchal (Paris: Pléiade, 1998), p. 69. Raitt and Castex see this poem as indebted to Villiers's *Véra*.
6 Paul Celan, *Collected Prose*, trans. Rosemarie Waldrop (Manchester: Carcanet, 1999), p. 12.